DETERMINED LOOK

Life Lessons of a Youth Football Coaching Legend

By: Three Year Letterman

 This is a work of satirical and hyperbolic fiction. Names, characters, businesses, products, places, schools, events, teams, locales, and incidents are either the products of the author's imagination or, in the case of actual businesses, persons, products, places, schools, teams, and locales, are used in a fictitious manner. With the exception of public figures and publicized events mentioned by name, any resemblance to actual persons, living or dead, or actual events is purely coincidental.

About the Author

Three Year Letterman is an athlete, a coach, a mentor, a friend, an essayist, a cultural critic, an intellectual, a football analyst, the consummate University of Georgia football fan, and an all-around badass. You can follow him on Twitter (@3YearLetterman), where his tweets have been enriching lives around the world. He and his youth football team will be profiled in the soon-to-be-released documentary *Three Year Letterman.*

"You look like you never lettered in shit."

- Three Year Letterman

Introduction

I am, to put it modestly, a youth football coaching legend. In the Northeast Georgia youth football circuit, I'm Nick Saban and Bill Belichick all wrapped into one.

In an era where we're increasingly told that the purpose of youth sports is to "build self-esteem," "teach teamwork," or "let the kids have fun," I'm part of the shrinking vanguard that still values winning above all else. I know about winning, because I've been doing it my entire life. And you don't have to take my word for it—the proof is emblazoned on the ring I wear for the high school football region championship (three-way tie) we won senior year. It's also found on my letter jacket, which I still wear proudly to this day. Stitched onto the jacket are three stripes signifying that I lettered for three years at wide receiver. For my career, I had twelve receptions for ninety-seven yards and one touchdown (a fumble recovery) in a Wing-T offense. But make no mistake about it, in 1996, I was the most devastating downfield blocker in the entire State of Georgia. I impart these talents on the next generation by coaching a youth football dynasty that I've built from the ground up.

My successes are not limited to the football field, however. As the supervisor for a home entertainment installation crew, I rake in $29.35 an hour plus bennies and a cell phone (which fits snugly in my custom leather belt holster). This income finances a lavish lifestyle. I currently live in an apartment complex with a pool, computer lab with free laser printing, and a refurbished Nautilus machine. I recently upgraded to a deluxe, "water view" corner unit apartment that overlooks the complex pond and its sometimes-functioning fountain. My apartment is adorned with a fully paid-off futon and a water bed that I purchased without financing. I have a credit card with a $4,500 limit and over $3,300 in my retirement account, despite being only thirty-nine. I've only declared bankruptcy once.

I project an image of success at all times. It's rare to find me not wearing a pair of freshly-pressed black jeans, wraparound Oakley sunglasses (even indoors), seven or eight pumps of Tim McGraw Southern Blend cologne, and, of course, a determined look on my face. I am above-average height, in good shape, and always have a fresh high and tight haircut like you see military members or police officers wearing. I spend thousands of dollars annually at Beef 'O' Brady's, where I watch most major sporting events with my youth football team's defensive coordinator (more on him in a minute).

I'm a die-hard University of Georgia Bulldogs football fan. While I didn't attend school there (dropped out of a much less renowned two-year college after three semesters when I realized I was smarter than all the professors and that college was a Ponzi scheme), no fan does more for the team's success. I have no qualms about barking at you, your children, or your aging grandparents if you're wearing another school's colors. I've given innumerable swirlies to opposing fans. Some call it over the top—I call it being "all in."

My sidekick in most of these endeavors is my best friend from high school. He serves as my youth football team's defensive coordinator. I refer to him as "my DC." In high school, he was an absolute wrecking ball of a middle linebacker and led the region in tackles and personal fouls our senior season. He dropped out of school and got his GED after getting (wrongly) passed over for defensive player of the year at the team awards banquet. His employment history and personal life have been a bit unstable. He hit rock bottom in November, 2013, when he caught a DUI arrest after being found during lunchtime passed out in the bushes near Hardee's. He's since gotten his life back on track and is now a proud Sonic employee. He drives a white Chrysler LeBaron convertible.

My DC stands about 5'8 and a powerful 220 pounds. He wears a "combover" style haircut, his face is often very red, and he has a tendency to breathe heavily. He usually wears his Sonic uniform, but when he's not in that, he's wearing "dad jeans" that are an inch or two too long and a pair of shabby-looking tennis shoes from the mid-'00s. He has a closet full of cheap-looking Georgia football jerseys and Atlanta Braves baseball jerseys.

A volatile, emotional, and unpredictable person, my DC can be furious one minute and crying the next. He's particularly prone to "meltdowns" when Georgia loses a game or a key player gets injured or suspended. Indeed, the loss to Auburn in 2013 is what prompted the aforementioned DUI arrest. He reads at a seventh-grade level and has virtually no understanding of history, politics, or the world outside of where he lives. However, he has a brilliant football mind and is our youth football team's unquestioned emotional leader.

People frequently come up to me, thank me for being a legend, and say, "Coach, how can I be like you?" The truth is that you probably can't. Nevertheless, I've written this book as an act of community service. I've given you a variety of youth football coaching and general life tips that—if followed—will allow you to one day experience some fraction of my life.

You're welcome.

Chapter 1

How to Theatrically Referee a Youth Basketball Game

When I'm not burnishing my reputation as a youth football coaching legend, I like to spend time giving back to the community, as all pillars of society should do. I serve as a youth baseball umpire (more on that later) and a substitute youth basketball referee when other referees are sick or otherwise cannot officiate. You'd think such a selfless act would draw universal praise from parents and coaches. But you'd be wrong. It's a sad commentary on our society that I've dealt with a constant chorus of complaints from angry parents and coaches that I am "showing up the kids" or "trying to draw attention to myself." If you decide to start officiating youth sports, make sure to block out these haters and never forget that you, as the official, are just as much a part of the game as the players.

With that backdrop, let's return to a chilly December night a few years ago. I was a substitute referee for a holiday basketball tournament championship game for the eleven and twelve-year-old division. It was a night that I'm sure no one in attendance will ever forget.

Before the game started, I instructed the coaches and players of both teams to gather around. I explained, as courtesy, that I'd be calling a much tighter game than the average referee.

They did not heed my warning. This one little turd pissed me off immediately because he did that stupid thing where he'd leave his shooting hand "hanging" after a shot. The third time he did it, I t-ed his ass up and waved off the three-point shot he'd just made. And that's when the complaints from parents and coaches started. Several requests to "just let the kids play" were met with similar technicals and the ejection of an assistant coach and elderly spectator. The parents also got upset because my double-dribble call is just to mock what the kid did.

Although they only play seven-minute quarters, the game took about two hours to complete given the number of fouls, travels, and three-second calls (I like to keep my lanes clear, so I use a two-second count rather than three seconds). The players continued to hand check even though I warned them it'd be an automatic foul. I called fifteen "carrying" calls in the first half alone until the players finally got the message that if their hand left the top of the ball, the whistle was blowing. The final carnage was over fifty free throws and half the starters fouled out by the beginning of the fourth quarter.

It actually ended up being a close, exciting game that was tied up with under a minute left. It was an electric atmosphere, and I knew I needed to do something in the waning seconds to take the things to another level and put my personal stamp on the game. So when one kid drove to the basket, he was pretty clearly blocked by an opposing player. But I decided to make a show-stopping charge call nonetheless. I did this move where I put my left hand behind my head and pointed the other way with my right hand three times. With each "point," I would slide forward and blow the whistle. After the final whistle blow, I just stared at the kid who committed the charge with a determined look on my face. It sent the crowd into a frenzy.

The team that was the beneficiary of the charge call came down and scored as the buzzer sounded to win the game. I got so caught up in the moment I ran down and jumped on top of their celebratory dog pile.

It got a touch dangerous after that. Several parents from the losing team were screaming at me and had to be physically restrained by the security guards. I went to high school with a few of them (all of whom, of course, never lettered in shit), so I just pointed to the three stripes on my letter jacket and got the hell out of there.

Chapter 2

How to Make the Shitty Players Quit

One of the more unfortunate recent developments in youth sports is the implementation of minimum, mandatory playing time for all players, no matter how useless. Equally disturbing, most leagues prohibit you from cutting players or kicking them off the team just because they suck. Unfortunately, I was unaware of this sickening concept when I became a youth football coach and drafted my first team. But now, I'm going to share a can't-miss strategy so you can avoid the same pitfalls.

There comes a point in every youth sports draft when all the useful players have been drafted. By that point, the only players left are ones who have nothing to contribute. My first season coaching, I mistakenly assumed that I could just bench their asses for the entire game, and then they'd either quit or benignly occupy space on the sidelines.

After the draft, though, I discovered the league had a "one quarter" rule. This rule requires every player to play at least one continuous quarter in every game. I'm always up for circumventing the rules when possible, but avoiding this one is difficult because the parents all want their sons to play. A couple of times during my first season I "completely forgot" about a particular player until there were ninety seconds left in the game and the outcome was no longer in doubt. But you can only get away with that excuse once or twice a season. In any event, the ultimate consequence of the "one quarter" rule is that terrible players aren't just useless tackling dummies; they're affirmative detriments to the team.

To solve this problem, I developed a truly revolutionary approach for the draft. Once the useful players are gone, most coaches will pick kids at random because they all suck anyway. That's what I did my first season because I didn't know any better. My second season coaching, we did a lot of research before the draft to identify those uniquely pathetic, weak-willed kids we thought we could make quit. This proved to be a stroke of genius, as we were able to purge the roster of nearly all useless players by mid-season.

But simply drafting weak-willed players is of little value if you can't follow through and rid your team of them. Thus, a critical weapon in any championship coach's arsenal is the ability to make the shitty kids quit voluntarily.

I personally prefer to try peaceful means at the outset. After identifying the players who have no prayer of helping us, we focus on trying to make those players quit through humiliation. My DC and other members of my coaching staff will mock their ineptitude and berate them in front of their teammates, which usually results in tears. I then play the role of the "good cop." I pull each useless player to the side, tell him in the most professional way possible that he's embarrassing himself, his teammates, and his entire family, and advise him that it would be best for all involved if he quits. That usually does the trick for fifty to seventy-five percent of players.

But when diplomatic means fail, I ratchet things up a bit. There are a variety of drills I've developed over the years that serve the dual purpose of punishing the decent players for poor play and making the weak-willed players quit. I've become particularly fond of the "Punt

Returns with No Fair Catches" drill, which is self-explanatory. It begins with putting the player I want to quit as the punt returner. I then put the biggest, meanest, hardest-hitting players as the "gunners" on the punt team and instruct them to obliterate the return man, preferably before the ball even reaches him. The "Kickoff Wedge Busting" drill is a similar, if less extreme, concept. (There technically are no live punts or kickoffs in youth football, but that's neither here nor there.) Other drills I like to use include running agility ropes on gravel and Oklahoma drills in the parking lot.

When all else fails, my last resort is to do everything I can to make the player's parents hate me. Insult their son, their child-rearing skills, their eduction, their profession, or their physical appearance—whatever it takes. I've made parents run gassers alongside their kids and participate in Oklahoma drills. I've arranged to have fictitious "unspoken" prayer requests made on their behalf at church with a vague reference to unnamed "demons" they are battling. But the one tactic I've become most fond of over the years is making incendiary posts on their

Facebook wall. It's amazing what you can accomplish with a well-placed "your son is useless" or "I wish there was a option for me to dislike this photo" or "you really look like shit in your new profile picture" post.

Chapter 3

How to Attend a High School Football Game and Post-Game Field Party in Style

Supporting your local high school football team ought to be a priority for anyone with a proper sense of community. I'm a devoted supporter of my high school and attend pretty much every game. But just as important as supporting the team is doing so in style.

It all begins with selecting the correct attire. If you're a former multi-year letterman like me, you should always wear your letter jacket to the game, regardless of the temperature. It's vital to send a message to everyone in attendance that you're an alumnus worthy of respect, not some special teams senior who only got a jacket because every senior gets one. If it's so hot that you're worried about passing out in the jacket, you can take it off and tie the arms around your neck like people sometimes do with sweaters at country clubs. For cool, crisp evenings, I like to go with a black mock turtleneck underneath my old high school football jersey, freshly pressed black jeans, and white LA Gears. It's a refined, yet intimidating, look. And I always finish off the look with seven or eight pumps of Tim McGraw Southern Blend cologne, which, like a foghorn, announces my presence to all in attendance.

I prefer to arrive a couple hours early so that I can tailgate in the school parking lot before the game. Once the game begins, I almost always go stand in the student section. I do my own play-by-play announcing and color commentary so that the students can have access to my knowledge, and you can tell they really appreciate that. During timeouts and changes of possession, I regale them with stories of my own high school playing days and re-enact some of my more memorable downfield blocks. I'm also not shy about loudly criticizing players, which sometimes leads to angry confrontations with their parents.

While the game itself is important, the post-game field parties are among the most important events of the annual social calendar. It's an incredible feeling of accomplishment to stride up to the party in your letter jacket as people look on with sheer awe. And I'm not sure there's a non-football activity that is more of an adrenaline rush than doing a keg stand while former and current students of your high school cheer and chant your name. If you haven't done that, you haven't lived.

Chapter 4

Supporting Your College Football Team

I am, without question, the most committed Georgia football fan you'll find. I once watched game highlights on my phone when I got bored during a co-worker's funeral. I refused to go to my sister's wedding because it conflicted with the spring game and she was marrying a Georgia Tech graduate. My enthusiasm for Georgia football has gotten me handcuffed, punched, tased, and pepper sprayed, but thankfully never arrested. I hitchhiked across the country to attend last year's Rose Bowl. My DC and I once pawned his girlfriend's son's laptop to finance tickets for a game. It truly just means more to me.

An ordinary fan lends their support, but I also lend my immense expertise and wisdom to the program. Sometimes the team has "open" fall camp practices that fans are able to attend. Several years back, I attended one, but immediately noticed that the wide receivers were not taking sharp enough angles on their slant routes. I began shouting instructions at them from the sideline and kept correcting the wide receiver coach's advice. I was asked to leave. I also use social media to either Tweet at or send Facebook messages to current Georgia coaches and players (at least the ones who haven't blocked me) with pointers for how they can improve.

I do a lot of film review. Each week, I re-watch Georgia's game and then either email or call the athletic department with strategic recommendations that I ask them to pass on to the staff. After the 2012 SEC Championship Game when we lost to Alabama, I made a tape of all of the plays where Alabama should have been called for a holding penalty. I provided voiceover commentary and used one of those markers that writes on the screen to point out the hold for each play. I sent the five-hour tape to the SEC offices and demanded reversal of the result. I also sent it to CBS for a potential *60 Minutes* episode. I've yet to get a definitive "no" from either, so I'm still holding out hope.

Yet, my impact as a fan is felt most greatly in my efforts to intimidate opposing fans. When I attend a Georgia game, I view it as my duty to make opposing fans as miserable as possible. It starts during the tailgate. If you're wearing the opposing team's colors, I'm going to come up to your tailgate, help myself to your food and alcohol, and then dare you to do anything about it. If I see you out walking around downtown Athens, I will come up to you, get in your face, bark at you, and do the "What's that coming down the track?" chant. I've done it to toddlers and World War II veterans alike. When the game is over and victory is in hand, I always head out to the upper-deck concourse to grab fleeing opposing fans and drag them into the bathroom for victory swirlies.

One of my biggest pet peeves, however, is when fellow Georgia "fans" start trying to intervene in these intimidation efforts and tell me that I'm "an embarrassment" and need to "show a little class." Those fans are just as bad—if not worse—than the opposing fans and therefore get the same treatment.

Chapter 5

Recruiting Replacements for Shitty Players

While I devote a lot of time before each youth football draft to collecting intelligence on potential players in order to make my draft picks as effective as possible, there are inevitable "busts" and other misfires. A successful youth football coach and his staff need to be prepared to pound the pavement mid-season to recruit replacements. And you have to be prepared to bend a few rules in the process.

My first year coaching, our offense was so poor to start the season that we recruited a replacement quarterback. I went to meet the kid and his father in the parking lot at Long John Silver's for a workout. While this was a league for nine and ten-year olds, it was pretty obvious when I met the kid that he was thirteen or fourteen. His voice was already changing, and he had tracings of a mustache. But he was only in the fourth grade, and his father assured me he just "looks old for his age." I decided to take the father at his word and didn't ask any further questions, even though I saw the son smoking a cigarette as I departed. "Don't ask, don't tell," I believe the policy was called. Not surprisingly, the kid ended up being an incredible quarterback playing against kids likely three to four years his junior.

The next season, my team had a similar dilemma. We used a high-round pick on this defensive lineman named Shane. He ended up being so useless and jumped offsides so often that we started calling him "Shane the Dumbass" in an attempt to humiliate him into playing better. But he only got worse. I therefore instructed my staff to hit the recruiting trail mid-season to find a replacement.

My DC eventually struck gold. One day, while working at Sonic, he began telling a patron about our youth football team's defensive issues (his manager had repeatedly warned him to stop this behavior after customer complaints, but to no avail), and the guy he was speaking with gave him a tip about a potential defensive lineman recruit with a rat tail. The kid was in juvie and then suspended for the first month of school after he attacked a librarian at the end of the prior school year. Evidently, he body slammed her after being informed that someone else had checked out the *Scary Stories to Tell in the Dark* series (he's not capable of reading the books, but is a big fan of the unforgettable and haunting illustrations). Under league rules, players are ineligible to play during a suspension. But with his suspension over, he was suddenly able to play. We ended up signing the kid later that evening after having him run some drills in the sporting goods aisle at Kmart. He became an unstoppable force on our defensive line.

Chapter 6

Reconsidering *Rudy*: Why Rudy was a Major Douche and Jamie O'Hara was Correct

In addition to being a legend on the football field, I'm a prolific essayist and cultural critic. My specialty is re-examining sports movies and documentaries from the past and then telling the hard truths about the messages those movies send. Let's start with the 1993 film *Rudy*.

I hate *Rudy*. I've probably watched the movie two dozen times in my life because I don't really watch non-football movies, and I get angrier and angrier with every viewing. If you haven't seen *Rudy*, let me bring you up to speed in a single sentence: Daniel "Rudy" Ruettiger, a shitty athlete from Joliet, Illinois with bad grades and a disrespectful attitude toward his father and brother, somehow ends up walking on at Notre Dame in the 1970's, sits in the dark and cries while holding a Notre Dame jacket, makes some meaningless tackle at the end of a game he never should have played in, and gets carried off the field.

I could write an entire book about the problems with *Rudy*—the shameless fetishization of Notre Dame, portraying Rudy's teacher as the "bad guy" for not letting Rudy crash a bus trip to Notre Dame for serious students, making a Notre Dame student seem heartless when she kicks Rudy out of the helmet-painting club (LOL) for lying about being a student, and portraying Dan Devine as a villain for actually doing his job (trying to win) and not wanting to play some walk-on loser who sucks. The list goes on and on. But today, I want to address the most disturbing aspect of Rudy's personality.

Anyone who played high school football almost certainly played with someone like Rudy. And we all hated him. He's the guy who shouts while lifting weights. He shows up to early-morning summer workouts and claims it's his "favorite part of the day." He asks the coach if the team can run extra gassers at the end of practice. He stays out on the practice field for an extra hour hitting the blocking sled. He tries to be a "coach on the field" and yells at his teammates for "not playing through the whistle." He makes a dramatic show of hitting his helmet in frustration when he misses a tackle, which is pretty much every play. He always has the defensive playbook under his arm and reads it alone at lunch. He makes awkward attempts to be friends with the coaches. But above all, he absolutely sucks as a football player and has no hope of ever contributing on the field.

In a just world, there would be no Rudys. High school coaches would have the ability and the willingness to run these losers off before they have a chance to poison practices with their earnestness and "hustling." But we do not live in a just world. We live in a world where this kind of behavior is not only tolerated, but celebrated. And the most shining example of that is *Rudy*.

There are countless examples of this nonsense in the movie, but one scene in particular stands out. It's Notre Dame's last practice of the season, and as best I can tell, the third string offense is scrimmaging against the scout team defense. In other words, who really gives a shit? It's a time to go through the motions and get done with practice. Instead, Rudy decides to act like Billy Badass and goes blowing through the line at full speed. He tackles running back Jamie

O'Hara, portrayed by Vince Vaughn. If Hollywood had any sense of fairness, O'Hara would have kicked Rudy's ass on the spot, and Notre Dame's head coach, Ara Parseghian, would have thrown Rudy off the team for good.

That doesn't happen. Instead, Parseghian self-righteously lectures O'Hara about his own lack of hustle and Rudy's "heart." He then unjustly demotes O'Hara to the "prep team" for doing the right thing.

It's a scene that makes me shake with rage during every viewing. It has, however, had some practical value. I show *Rudy* to my youth football team every year and explain that if any of them act like Rudy, they'll be forced to wade through the copperhead-infested creek in the woods behind the football field. If Ara Parseghian had done the same, Notre Dame might have more than one national championship since the '70s.

Chapter 7

How to Dominate a Deposition

If you're like me and prefer to live at the edges of what society deems "legal," there inevitably will come a time when you must give a deposition or provide trial testimony. When that day comes, it's important that you understand how to dominate the examining attorney.

Several years ago, my DC had to give a deposition. It was a simple slip and fall that he witnessed at the mall the prior August. He was coming out of watching *Transformers 4* for the second time (to catch anything he "might have missed" during the first viewing). The person who fell sued the mall for failing to clean up spilled nacho cheese that caused her to slip. I guess she pulled a muscle or sustained some other meaningless injury that wouldn't warrant sitting out a play on my youth football team, let alone merit a lawsuit. But I digress.

Although the mall's incident report listed him as an eyewitness, my DC had been drinking a handle of bottom-shelf whiskey throughout the movie and was absolutely hammered when the fall happened. He eventually blacked out that night and had no memory of what transpired. For most people that wouldn't be a problem. But for him, being intoxicated violates the terms of his probation, which could result in a multi-month stay in the county lock-up.

After appearing in court and unsuccessfully demanding that the presiding judge "squash" the subpoena, my DC agreed to appear at the plaintiff's attorney's office for the deposition. The deposition immediately got off to a rocky start when my DC refused to answer a preliminary question about his current residential address. The correct answer was "none" (another probation violation), but he refused to answer due to "identity theft" concerns. The attorneys also had to get the judge on the phone to instruct my DC to stop making evidentiary objections (he prepared for the deposition by watching several episodes of the television show *Suits*) and to stop saying "off the record" before he would start answering a question.

Eventually, the plaintiff's attorney asked one too many questions, and my DC just lost it and went after him. The other attorney, the court reporter, and a member of the janitorial staff had to restrain my DC from attacking the plaintiff's attorney. The deposition was terminated. Building security was called, and they forcibly escorted my DC out of the building. He shouted incoherently about his "due process rights" the entire walk out.

The good news is that the attorneys for both sides were so shaken up over the whole incident that they decided not to reconvene my DC's deposition or call him as a trial witness. And, the deposition ended before my DC had to answer any questions that would have required him to divulge that he was absolutely obliterated at the time of the slip and fall. So he was able to come out of the whole ordeal relatively unscathed.

Here's an excerpt from the transcript:

Attorney: And where do you currently work?

DC: Objection. Calls for hearsay and violates the best evidence rule.

Attorney: Sir, that is not a valid objection, and even it was, this is just a deposition, so you still have to answer the question.

DC: Off the record.

Attorney: We've been over this several times. You cannot just say "off the record" whenever I ask a question to avoid answering the question. I'll ask the court reporter to repeat the pending question. You need to answer it on the record.

[Question read back]

DC. Objection, calls for speculation.

Attorney: This needs to stop. Please answer the question on the record.

DC: Off the record.

Attorney: Alright, I've had enough of this. Let's get the judge on the phone again.

DC: Go right ahead. If you think I'm scared of the federal government, think again.

Attorney: Sir, please return to your side of the table.

Chapter 8

"Adjusting" Birth Certificate and Residency Information

Official documentation can be a roadblock for getting the best youth football players. After all, if a kid exceeds the age limit or technically lives outside of your district, he isn't allowed to play for your team. Most coaches would just accept the fact that a player is not eligible due to age or residency issues and move on. A legend like myself, however, views paperwork not as an insurmountable barrier, but as a minor roadblock to be driven around.

That brings us to perhaps the most overlooked component of a youth football dynasty—good legal counsel. To assist my team with its inevitable legal issues, I hired my cousin, a local workers' compensation attorney with a fledgling solo practice. He went to a law school I've never heard of and then failed the bar three times before passing. In exchange for becoming the team's legal counsel, I agreed to give him unlimited use of my parents' time share in Westminster, South Carolina and above-ground pool during the summer. He's no stranger to ethical complaints, so I knew he was right for the job.

He's been invaluable in counseling me through thorny legal situations, particularly those involving documentation. I don't want to go into details in case league officials or law enforcement officers are reading this, but my cousin was instrumental in laying the groundwork for this one kid named Cody—who technically did not live in the district—to play for our team. My cousin filed some paperwork to change Cody's official residence to a local campground that is located within our district. There was some truth to that statement, as Cody occasionally slept at the campground when his step dad kicked him out of the house for getting into the liquor supply. "Plausible deniability," my cousin called it.

Chapter 9

How to Catch Foul Balls and Home Runs at a Major League Baseball Game

It's no secret that I'm a very big Braves fan. I've had a lot of fun at Braves games over the years—shoving Yankees fans into the urinal "troughs" at old Atlanta-Fulton County Stadium, pouring beer on the head of an eight-year-old Mets fan at Turner Field when the Braves hit a home run, and unsuccessfully attempting to go down onto the field and confront the umpires after the "infield fly rule" debacle in the 2012 wild card game. But one of my primary goals when I attend a Braves game is to catch a foul ball or home run.

It begins with the attire, as it's important to get in a baseball mindset if you're going to snag a ball. While I usually wear shorts and a braided belt to Braves games due to the heat, I pair up those items with a Braves jersey and baseball spikes (and I mean actual metal spikes, not cheap rubber cleats). I then finish off the look with a Braves hat, batting gloves, and a first baseman's mitt (although a catcher's mitt or normal glove will also do). It's important to wear the glove the entire game, because you never know when an errant ball will come your way.

Back in the mid-2000's I went to a game at Turner Field and sat in the outfield. I got there early for batting practice, only to discover I was sitting behind a group of elementary schoolers. While that might have stopped or discouraged the average fan from trying to catch a ball, it certainly did not dissuade me. When a Braves player launched a batting practice home run that was heading right at the elementary school group, I calmly stood up, reached my glove over their heads, snagged the ball, and put it in my pocket.

As I began to high five all the people around me, one of the elementary school chaperones angrily confronted me and accused me of "stealing the ball from a bunch of kids." I told her that she really should be thanking me. After all, the kids all looked like a bunch of unathletic losers who couldn't catch a ball if their lives depended on it, so by reaching over their heads and catching the ball, I likely prevented a serious injury to one of them.

Sadly, we live in a world where heroism is not always recognized, and I was asked by several other fans to apologize and return the ball. I refused, kept the ball, and eventually sold it on eBay for a tidy thirteen-dollar profit.

Chapter 10

Fostering Ties with the Local Sheriff's Department

While having a great attorney for your youth football team is important, it's also vital to develop ties with local law enforcement. If you're doing things the right way, either your players or your coaches will invariably have brushes with the law. And when that happens, you need to be able to call in a favor. Fortunately for me, I know a deputy who works for the local sheriff's department. He was, at one point, several hundred dollars in debt to me from bets we'd placed on pinewood derby races. I had to call in that debt in a major way a few years ago.

We took our youth football team to a haunted house a few days before Halloween as something of a team-building outing. My DC is afraid of almost nothing (we're talking about a guy who once leg dropped a family of rattlesnakes on a dare), but he's absolutely terrified of the paranormal. He had night terrors and refused to use VCRs for a good two years after he watched

The Ring. When we arrived at the haunted house, he was trying to maintain his composure in front of the players, but I could tell he was extremely nervous. His face was beet red, and he was sweating profusely.

We went into a dark room that had ominous organ music playing and a vampire laying in a casket. My DC thought the vampire was only a mannequin and went over to the casket with a couple of players. As he and the players were leaning over the casket, the vampire suddenly rose up. My DC yelled and reflexively punched the vampire right in the face, knocking him out cold.

Chaos ensued. A couple of security guards swooped in and grabbed my DC by his arm, but he used his free hand to throw punches at the guard dressed like Freddy Krueger (the *Nightmare On Elm Street* series also gives him nightmares). Meanwhile, someone attempted to get the vampire to regain consciousness with smelling salts. Turns out the vampire was a fifteen-year-old high school kid who ended up with very prominent black eye and a concussion.

The police were called, but thankfully we had my cousin the workers' compensation attorney there to intervene. He argued that the vampire provoked my DC, causing him to react involuntarily. After I dropped the name of my buddy the deputy sheriff and mentioned his pinewood derby gambling debt, the responding officers realized they were in over their heads and left without arresting my DC. They said they would re-visit the issue if the vampire kid decided to press charges.

On our way out, one of my assistant coaches threatened to drive a wooden stake into the vampire kid's heart if he said anything more to the police about the incident. I'll concede the threat was borderline, but I always encourage the staff to err on the side of going too far. And with good reason, because we didn't hear a word about the incident thereafter.

Chapter 11

Getting Revenge on an Old Adversary

People often come up to me and ask, "Coach Letterman, how on earth were you not a four-year letterman in high school?" It's a great question, and the story behind it is one that still makes me shake with rage. Yet, recounting that tale teaches the value of holding grudges and exacting revenge years after the original slight.

My freshman year of high school, it was evident to pretty much anyone with a functioning brain that I should be a starting wide receiver. The guy I was competing with for the spot was some loser senior named Todd who'd never taken a meaningful snap. Todd was slow, gangly, couldn't block, and had the appearance of wearing invisible iron mittens whenever he tried to catch the ball. Making matters worse, he was one of those dumbasses who "went all out" on every play in practice and treated basic warm-ups like they were the goddamn Olympics. You'd often see him on the field after practice running routes and throwing the tether ball by himself, as if that was going to do any good. He was like a more pathetic version of Rudy. No doubt he had a shelf at home full of "Hustle" and "Most Improved Player" awards.

Unfortunately, my head coach had a loser's mindset. He acknowledged that I was a vastly superior athlete, but expressed concern about my "attitude," "excessive use of profanity," "constant attempts to change the play in the huddle," and "frequent questioning of the coaching staff's coaching abilities." Todd, on the other hand, had "put in his time" and "done everything we've asked him to do." So I had to spend that season standing on the sideline, not lettering, and watching Todd shit the bed on every offensive series. It was infuriating, and after the season was over, I got the head coach fired by claiming he was pilfering football equipment and school supplies (not true).

Flash forward about two decades, and Todd is a bank teller and has a son who—surprise, surprise—completely sucks at youth football. Although my employer offers direct deposit, I still demand a paper check so I can march into the bank every other Friday in my letter jacket, storm up to Todd's station, and toss the signed check down. I then stare at him with a determined look on my face while he absorbs the fact that I rake in $29.35 an hour plus bennies and a cell phone (which I make sure to display prominently in my custom leather belt holster when I go in the bank). Revenge is indeed a dish best served cold.

Chapter 12

Developing a Practice Itinerary

All great youth football coaches must run an organized and rigorous practice that, quite frankly, scares people. Here's an outstanding practice itinerary that I developed for the season's first practice. As you'll see, it's perfectly calibrated to weed out useless players and their parents.

Practice Itinerary – July 31, 2018

Note – Practice is *closed* to all parents and the media. I will address the media when practice concludes.

4:15-4:45: Custom Sizing for the Weight Vests in Which the Players Must Practice

4:45-5:00: Warmups

5:00-6:30: Oklahoma Drills in the Parking Lot (might want to bring extra thick knee pads and elbow guards)

6:30-6:45: Coach Letterman's Lecture Series, "The Honor Roll: Who Cares?"

6:45-7:30: Punt Returns with No Fair Catches Drill

7:30-8:00: Mandatory Fist Fighting with Teammates

8:00-8:15: Coach Letterman's Lecture Series, "Darwinism: Why Most People are Destined to be Losers Who Never Lettered in Shit"

8:15-8:45: Team Building Exercise—Wading Through the Copperhead-Infested Creek Behind the Field (bring swimwear; I don't want to risk snake venom staining our jerseys or equipment)

8:45-9:00: Coach Letterman's Press Conference (No questions allowed)

9:15-10:30: Dinner Meetings With Parents of Useless Players Who Should Probably Quit (Parents to pay the tab)

Chapter 13

Staying in Game-Ready Condition

A true multi-year high school football letterman, like me, never retires. I stay in game-ready shape should the call of duty ever come. At thirty-nine, I'm every bit as athletic as I was as a high school senior. If anything, I'm a more devastating downfield blocker now.

How do I do this? I'll tell you this—it isn't by wasting a bunch of money on a gym membership. I do my training on the football field. Every morning, I rise at dawn, put on my old high school jersey and football cleats, and head out to the local high school football field for my morning training session.

I start off by running stadiums and doing up-downs. Then, I run all kinds of wide receiver routes and shout out a hypothetical play-by-play radio call as I catch one game-winning touchdown after another. I then conclude by hitting the blocking sled and setting up some tackling dummies so that I can practice my downfield blocking.

Not only does this routine keep me in game-ready shape, but it inspires others. Oftentimes, when I'm crack blocking a tackling dummy to the ground or diving to catch an invisible game-winning touchdown in the back of the end zone, I'll look up and see students who are just arriving to school, looking down on the field with looks of pure awe and respect.

Chapter 14

Reconsidering Jonathan Moxon: How *Varsity Blues* Gave America its First Millennial

1999 was a unique point in American history. It's that tiny sliver of time that post-dates the advent of the internet, yet pre-dates 9/11, the Great Recession, the smart phone, and the rise of social media. The American high school experience would be radically different in 2009 than it was in 1999. And, if the Great American Novel were a movie, it would be *Varsity Blues*, which perfectly captures the zeitgeist of the late '90s.

The premise of *Varsity Blues* is simple. In West Canaan, Texas—a fictional town that embodies pre-Great Recession middle America—legendary high school football coach Bud Kilmer is embarking on his quest for a twenty-third district title and third state title. The supposed protagonist is Jonathan Moxon, the "smart" back-up to two-time all-state quarterback and Florida State commitment Lance Harbor. To the untrained eye, the movie is the tale of an idealistic football player (Moxon) who sees through West Caanan's misplaced priorities and backwards thinking and rallies his teammates to revolt against Kilmer—whom the filmmakers would have you believe is an old-fashioned and abusive coach. Yet, the conflict between Moxon and Kilmer is about so much more than just those two characters.

In Moxon and Kilmer, we see the values of two completely different types of Americans. If we assume that *Varsity Blues* depicts the 1999 football season, that would mean Jonathan Moxon was born in 1981 or 1982, and therefore was one of the first members of the Millennial Generation. But putting the technical birthdate definition aside, there can be no doubt that Jonathan Moxon was the first on-screen character to embody all of the Millennial traits—weak, self-entitled, unwilling to listen, blaming others for his actions, disrespectful to authority figures, etc. Kilmer, on the other hand, was part of a now-disappearing generation that valued hard work, respect, and a bunch of other vague but noble-sounding terms. You sympathized with one character or the other; there was no middle ground.

My lasting criticism of the movie is that it incorrectly portrays Moxon as the "hero." In so doing, *Varsity Blues* sent a message to an impressionable generation of moviegoers that they should strive to be just like Jonathan Moxon. It therefore should come as no surprise that when this generation started to hit the workforce a decade later, we were flooded with think pieces on how to "deal" with this awful group of people. This essay explains why we have *Varsity Blues* to thank for that, because it created the Millennial Generation.

Our first real insight into who Moxon is comes a few minutes into the movie, during the pep rally scene. While Kilmer delivers a rousing speech to the crowd and introduces Lance Harbor, where is Moxon? Standing with his teammates to show his support? Of course not. He's standing off the side with his girlfriend, sulking about the attention Harbor is getting, and making a disgusting and unfunny joke at Kilmer's expense. So the movie establishes very quickly that Moxon is not a team player.

The next noteworthy scene involving Moxon comes during that night's game against Bingville, where we see his dishonesty for the first time. With his team trying to put the game away in the fourth quarter, Moxon is sitting on the bench away from his teammates and using a playbook to cover up the fact that he's reading a novel during the game. I'd also be remiss if I didn't take a second to talk about the book Moxon is reading, "The Slaughterhouse Five" by Kurt Vonnegut. Along with "The Catcher in the Rye," this is the book that every pseudo-intellectual, high school Millennial for the next two decades will lie and claim as their favorite. "It works on so many levels" they'll tell you, without ever identifying what those other levels might be. I've never read it, but I'm sure it sucks just based on the people I know who like it.

Also, while it doesn't technically involve Moxon, a scene from the party after the Bingville game ominously foreshadows the Millennial generation's lack of respect for the past. During that party, we are introduced to a former West Canaan football player from the class of 1980. By any objective measure, this is a man who deserves our respect. Despite having graduated from the school almost two decades before, he still attends games, wears his letter jacket, and "never miss[es]" the post-game parties.

And how is this pillar of the community repaid for loyally supporting the team? With Charlie Tweeder violently striking him in the genitals with a whiffle ball bat while other students laugh hysterically and videotape him writhing in agony on the ground. There's no doubt that if this occurred in 2018, that footage would be up on social media within the hour. All in all, it's an absolutely disgusting scene that the filmmakers pass off as comedy.

From there, we as the audience are treated to a never-ending string of Moxon's selfish and otherwise awful behavior. He intentionally breaks his father's nose with a football. He organizes an all-night drinking party involving the team's best players the night before a game to sabotage the season. He and Billy Bob get heavily intoxicated and use firearms on a youth football field to destroy public property, yet blame Kilmer for their conduct. He pouts like a baby when Kilmer threatens to imperil his scholarship to Brown and considers quitting on his teammates. He attempts to substitute his own judgment for that of medical professionals when he stops a trainer from administering a career-saving injection to running back Wendell Brown's knee. And finally, he quits during the middle of the team's most important game of the year and then organizes a coup to topple a confirmed Texas high school coaching legend.

If there's anything more "Millennial" than all that, I'm unaware of it.

Almost twenty years later, we continue to fret about why Millennials act they way they do. Thousands of articles, speeches, books, and studies have all been devoted to exploring this issue. Being a "generational consultant" has become an actual profession.

And who do we have to thank for that? The filmmakers who announced to an entire generation that this toxic behavior was not only acceptable, but was, in Moxon's words, "heroic." In short, *Varsity Blues* introduced America to its first Millennial, and we as a society have been paying the price ever since.

Chapter 15

Turning the Local School System from Adversary to Co-Conspirator

One of my biggest complaints about the youth football league in which I coach is that it has grossly overstepped its bounds. Although run by the parks and recreation department, the league requires all players to maintain a "C average" to be eligible to play. The players must furnish their report card each semester for inspection. And if players miss school or are suspended, they're not allowed to participate in a game or practice that same day. It's a disgusting abuse of power, but one I have to live with for the time being.

As a result, it's important that any burgeoning youth football coaching legend foster ties with the local school system. As you can probably imagine, I'm not without enemies at the local elementary school. I ask my players to stop doing most of their homework during the fall so that they can focus on football, and I encourage their parents to hold them out of school on game days. This offends a lot of teachers.

But as with any organization, the school system has diamonds in the rough. Perhaps my youth football team's biggest outside ally is the vice principal of the elementary school that my players attend. His name is Pete, and he's been of immense value to us.

At one point, we had a couple of players who had major disciplinary problems or were on the verge of academic ineligibility, so we were looking for some inside help. We were eventually able to work out an agreement with Pete under which he agreed to turn a blind eye to disciplinary problems and to "adjust" grades when necessary. In return, twice a month, we buy him beer and all the wings he can consume at Hooters. He also gets four free VIP passes to the local gentleman's club every quarter.

Pete may not fit within society's pre-conceived notion of a "passionate" educator, but he's done more to positively influence the lives of students than 99% of teachers out there. And it's all because he understands that these players learn far more on a football field than they ever will listening to some teacher yap about the War of 1812.

Chapter 16

How to Umpire a Youth Baseball Game

During the spring, I umpire youth baseball games for the parks and recreation department. And I take that job very, very seriously.

The foundation for any successful umpire is the development of a show-stopping strike three call. I usually go out to the baseball field by myself before the season starts to perfect the call. My trademark move involves a 180 degree turn and this violent arm action like I'm cranking an ailing lawnmower. I also utilize a somewhat unorthodox approach, as I make calls that I know technically aren't "correct" to exact justice, create drama, draw attention to myself, or advance some other noble aim. For instance, I've called players safe for making productive outs. I've called players out who clearly were safe if I felt they'd gotten a lucky hit. I call balks even though there are no balks in youth baseball (nor do I really know what a balk is) just to keep the pitchers on edge. It's an approach that rubs many the wrong way, but I firmly believe it's the way of the future.

Perhaps my most memorable moment as an umpire came during a game when I was the third-base umpire. The night had been mostly quiet out on the base paths, and I hadn't really had a chance to make any calls. But late in the game, there finally was a play where a player hit a ball into the gap and was trying to stretch a double into a triple. The throw was coming into third and it looked like it was going to be a bang-bang play. I was so amped up that I went into my "out" call before third baseman even caught the ball. I did this move where I step forward and jab with my left hand and then violently cross with my right.

Unfortunately, I had a lot more momentum than I thought, so it carried me past third base and into field of play. The runner came in much higher than I anticipated and I accidentally clipped his chin with the high school football region championship ring (three-way tie) on my right hand. Also, the runner clearly was safe, but that's neither here nor there.

Of course, the kid acted like a total baby about the whole thing and his parents were very upset. I blamed both of them and his coaches for not teaching the kid how to slide properly. I told them if they didn't agree, they could meet me in the parking lot after the game for a little lesson on proper sliding. They didn't take me up on that.

Chapter 17

Post-Game Handshakes

I do not permit my youth football players to fraternize with the enemy. And for us, the enemy is anyone who plays for another football team. I forbid my players from talking to students at their school who play for another team, even if they are family or friends. We give no quarter to the enemy on my team.

That brings us to post-game handshakes. In my view, post-game handshakes went out of style with powdered wigs and Victorian corsets. It's a silly formality from a bygone era that belongs in the dust bin of history. Yet, this awful practice continues to be a sports staple, particularly at the youth level, where people praise stupid things like "sportsmanship" and "class." When my youth football team has just finished embarrassing another team and running up the score, I am not going to lie and pretend it was a "good game." Thus, I have implemented an absolute ban on post-game handshakes, with the lone exception being when the handshake is a subterfuge for taunting or fighting our defeated opponent.

I once had a player on my team who violated this rule. He went to shake the hands of some friends and a relative on a team we'd just defeated. I was absolutely livid when I saw him consorting with the enemy. The next game, as soon as the final horn sounded, one of my assistant coaches pulled the kid to the side, applied superglue to his hands, and pressed them together so that it literally would be impossible for the kid to shake hands with the opposing team. He eventually had to go to a doctor's office to have his hands separated, but he never again tried to shake hands with the opposing team, so everything worked as planned.

Chapter 18

How to Tactfully Interrupt a Theatre Performance to Announce a Georgia Football Commitment

As a man of great taste and sophistication, I am a patron of the arts. Yet, it's important to remind those involved in theatre, painting, or something similar that they stand several pegs beneath football players and especially coaches on the social ladder.

I was able to make that point loud and clear last December, when I attended a local theatre production of "A Christmas Carol." I was impeccably attired in a recently-purchased white dinner jacket, black turtleneck, black jeans, and white LA Gears. Unfortunately, a very important high school offensive lineman that Georgia was recruiting was set to announce his decision that night during the middle of the performance.

But I came prepared. The commitment was being live streamed on Facebook, so when the time came, I whipped out my phone, put in my earbuds (so as not to disturb other attendees), and tuned in. A couple of people sitting nearby gave me strange looks, but I silently mouthed "I'm listening to the commitment ceremony" and pointed to my phone so that they knew there was a good reason for what I was doing.

Once the player announced that he was going to Georgia, I stood up, asked the crowd for a few moments of their attention, and said, "Ladies and Gentlemen, I am very pleased to announce that one of the country's best offensive linemen has just decided to be a Dawg!" I then started barking, and several fellow Georgia fans in attendance broke out into applause. The cast, however, was aghast. The theatre manager came over and tried to make me leave, but I caused a scene by loudly complaining that the cast members' British accents sucked. The guy playing the Ghost of Christmas Past started yelling at me from the stage to be quiet, and I told him I'd sit down as soon as he figured out how to pronounce "water" like an actual Brit. To get me to stop, the manager eventually let me stay with a stern warning. But the message to all in attendance was loud and clear—the show must always stop for Georgia football.

Chapter 19

Loyalty Oaths

Loyalty is the cornerstone of our society. I require each of my youth football players to pledge their undying and unflinching loyalty to the team. The team must supersede all other obligations, and it's best that any youth football coach get this point across to the players at the outset. In my experience, the best way to achieve this is through requiring the players to sign a loyalty oath. Below is an example of what I've given my team:

Parents,

As you know, fall practice starts tomorrow. Here is the Loyalty Oath. Please have your son read and sign (actually, I don't give a hoot in hell if they read it or are even capable of reading as long as they sign). An "X" will do.

Best,

Coach Letterman

LOYALTY OATH

I ____________, do hereby pledge my complete and undying loyalty to Coach Letterman and my youth football team. I accept that my obligations to the team supersede all others, including those to my family, school, friends, and church.

I promise to rid myself of all distractions. If I have pets, I will arrange to have them dropped off at the humane society by the end of this week. If I have video games, I will toss them into the garbage. I will burn all books, magazines, and newspapers in my house. If I have younger siblings, I will arrange to have them stay elsewhere for the next three months, so as to minimize the chance of contracting an infectious disease. I will quit all clubs, sports, and other activities. Homework is now a hobby, not an obligation. My real homework is reviewing the playbook, which I will do for at least ninety minutes every night. If I'm currently on the Honor Roll, I promise to be off of it by the end of the semester.

I promise to follow every order I receive from the coaching staff without question. Their instructions take precedent over conflicting instructions from my parents. If asked by a coach to attack an opposing player, teammate, referee, or aging family member, I will do so. If asked to walk into oncoming traffic, I will do so, because I trust the coaches completely.

So Sworn:

____

Chapter 20

Teaching Tee Ball Players Not to be Scared of the Ball

Although baseball is not my primary sport, given my coaching reputation in the local market, I've been brought in as a consultant by a couple of tee ball coaches to teach their players not to be afraid of the ball.

Teaching this skill is a multi-step process. I start out with fairly standard infield practice. I have the six and seven-year olds line up around the infield grass, and I then proceed to hit tee balls on the ground at them as hard as I possibly can. The kids who get in front of the ball and knock it down like men get the okay and stay on the field. The crying losers who do not get in front of the ball are ushered out to the parking lot to ramp things up a bit.

I start off with the same drill in the parking lot, except I use baseballs instead of tee balls. I require the players to stand about ten yards away from me, and I hit ground balls at them. I usually take some rocks and scatter them in front of the players to add an element of randomness to how the ball bounces. You typically have several players who actually do get in front of the ball because they are afraid of what awaits them if they don't.

Their fears are well-founded. The next step is to ratchet things up to what I call "DEFCON 1," and it requires the participation of a couple of other coaches. The goal at that point is to get rid of the remaining kids, because they clearly don't have what it takes to play for a championship tee ball team.

We line up the remaining players against a brick wall in the parking lot. Three or four of us—the "Firing Squad"—then stand about ten yards away with bats and a bucketful of golf balls. I then announce to the players that they have ten seconds to run away and quit voluntarily, or we will start simultaneously hitting the golf balls at them. Not a single player has ever stuck around long enough for the first ball to be hit, so that method has proven 100% effective in running off the useless players.

Once that's done, you return to the field and see what you've got left. Inevitably, it will be a tough, championship-minded group of six and seven-year-old kids who aren't afraid of the ball. If that isn't what tee ball is all about, I don't know what is.

Chapter 21

Offensive Strategy: Three Knees and Punt

My first season coaching, our offense was absolutely abysmal before I recruited the likely overage quarterback. Our defense, on the other hand, was almost impossible to move the ball on. Once we got a lead, the biggest threat to losing was not our immovable defense, but our turnover-prone offense. There are no live punts in my youth football league. Instead, a team can elect to "punt" on fourth down. The officials just move the ball forty yards down the field, and the possession changes. So there's no danger of getting a punt blocked or otherwise turning the ball over if you elect to punt on fourth down.

My understanding of this wrinkle gave birth to an innovative strategy. Once we got a lead on the other team, no matter how early or small the lead, I would immediately instruct our offense to go into "Three Knees and Punt" mode. The strategy is self-explanatory—the ball is snapped, and the quarterback takes a knee. We do that three times in a row, "punt" the ball to the other team, and let our defense win the game. It made us unbeatable with a lead.

You would think such a brilliant strategy would be met with widespread acclaim. Sadly, it was not. Parents of the players on my team started whining and imploring me to “let the kids play.” Opposing coaches threw tantrums. Referees and league officials told me this strategy “isn’t consistent with the spirit of the rules or the spirit of youth football in general,” like I give a shit about the “spirit” of anything. I pulled out the league rulebook, handed it to them, and told them to get the hell out of my face unless they could point me to a rule banning the strategy. They could not, and the strategy continued.

Chapter 22

Reconsidering *Last Chance U*: Why the Fight Between Buddy Stephens and the Referee is Everything that is Good and Right about America

Netflix's *Last Chance U* is a remarkable documentary that released its third brilliant season earlier this year. For those who don't know, the first two seasons of *Last Chance U* chronicled the 2015 and 2016 seasons of East Mississippi Community College. EMCC is coached by Buddy Stephens, a rotund man with a goatee, multiple championship rings, badass wraparound blade sunglasses, and a short temper. He's one of the few college coaches I'd be honored to have join my youth football team's coaching staff.

The series has many great moments, but my favorite comes in the first season. The moment is innocuous—EMCC is blowing out an opponent 31-7 in the fourth quarter. But out of nowhere, greatness ensues. Coach Stephens begins to say something to a sideline official, which leads to an argument, a shoving match, and the throwing of a clipboard and a punch.

It's a wonderful moment. In an era where far too many people treat sports like a hobby, we have two true American heroes coming to blows over some meaningless dispute at the end of a game that is no longer in doubt. These are two men who are clearly committed to winning and every other value we as Americans should cherish.

But this event brings to light a nationwide problem: the lost, noble art of fist fighting in this country. Fist fighting is the oldest and most effective means of dispute resolution. It is the original jury verdict. It is the original mediation. And it doesn't involve a bunch of lawyers getting paid a bunch of money. It's quick, efficient, and effective. The fight between Coach Stephens and the official was over in less than a minute, and it didn't cost anyone a penny. Court cases drag on for years.

Our country would undoubtedly be a much better place if we required our elected officials to settle disagreements by fighting one another. Can you imagine how much more efficiently the government would run if members of Congress were required to resolve disagreements by fighting one another? Instead of running off to the nearest cable news program to cry on the air about how mean their opponent is, they would be required to meet up in front of the Lincoln Memorial at dawn to settle their score. And to the victor goes the spoils.

Or what if there was no such thing as "dissents" in Supreme Court opinions? Dissent should consist of the dissenting justices confronting the majority in their chambers and duking it out. The prevailing group writes the opinion, and the losers must sign on. Just like God and Charles Darwin intended.

That's a long way of saying this country would be in a hell of a lot better shape if, instead of Mitch McConnell and Chuck Schumer, we had Buddy Stephens and a football referee as the majority and minority leaders of the U.S. Senate, settling every policy debate with their fists rather than empty words.

Chapter 23

Developing an "Academics" Protocol

If you're a youth football coach, it's important to communicate your expectations to players and parents alike. I recommend developing an "academics" protocol that you can send to parents at the beginning of the season to ensure they understand where their priorities should lie. Below is the protocol I handed out for this season:

Fall, 2018 "Academics" Protocol

Dear Parents,

As you should know by now, I require my players to devote all of their efforts to football. Unfortunately, the league continues to cling to the outdated notion that your sons need to maintain a "C" average to be eligible to play. Below is a guide that you can use to best "balance" football with academics to ensure your son stays eligible, but is not unnecessarily distracted by school.

Subjects

- **History** – Irrelevant. Our team is focused on the future, not the past.
- **Language Arts** – Can your son read the playbook? Can he understand the play calls? If so, he doesn't need it.
- **Math** – Mildly useful. Your son needs to know how to count to four, how a descending clock works, and how to follow a snap count. The rest is pointless.
- **Science** – LOL.
- **Art and Music** – LOLOLOLOLOL.
- **Gym** – Most important class. A great setting for physically dominating and intimidating opposing players.

Other Pointers

- **Tests/Quizzes** – Sit beside a smart classmate and copy.
- **Papers** – Find a paper bank online and purchase one.
- **Standardized Tests** – Skip. They have nothing to do with eligibility.
- **Clubs/After-School Activities** – Prohibited.

- **Homework** – You should spend 85% of your normal homework time studying the playbook.

Chapter 24

Attending a High School Basketball Game

I'm normally not much of a basketball guy, but I think it's important to make an appearance or two each year at high school basketball games and leave the same impact that I do for football games. A few years back, I decided to attend a game where my high school was playing our rival, and I gave the fans a show they won't soon forget.

The student section is situated directly behind the home team's bench, so I was only a row or two up from the players and the coaches. The head coach is a guy named Darren. He was a grade above me in high school and was one of those losers who rode the pine in basketball and only got a letter jacket because they give them to all seniors. Darren would also get upset with me and my DC during pick-up games for playing "overly aggressive" defense and elbowing him in the throat on rebounds. We've had testy exchanges on each other's Facebook walls over the last few years, so there's some history there.

I should have known it was going to be a difficult night when they were announcing the starting lineups. Every time they would announce a player for the opposing team, I would do my signature clap-clap-clap-clap-clap "OVER-RATED!" chant. The students I was sitting beside all thought it was great, but Darren and the school principal asked me to "show some class" and stop. The most disturbing part is that the principal had a clear view of the three stripes on my letter jacket and still decided to treat a distinguished alumnus with disrespect.

Once the game started, it was clear that the referees were being way too loose with the rules and allowing players to camp out in the lane. Whenever I saw an opposing player enter the lane, I loudly yelled "One! Two! Three!" into the plastic megaphone they gave me when I arrived. Darren told me I was "distracting the players" and asked me to stop.

By that point the game was starting to get away from us, and I was noticing serious defects in our players' defensive fundamentals. So I decided to take matters into my own hands. While Darren was over at the scorer's table during a timeout, I went down to the court and starting giving the players instructions and a physical demonstration on how to take a charge. Darren got really pissed when he saw that and called the security guard over. The security guard told me I could either move sections or leave, so I decided just to get the hell out of there and get an early start on the post-game field party. I pointed to my region championship ring (three-way tie) and told Darren he'd never get one of those and that I hoped he got fired. I received a standing ovation from the students on my way out.

Chapter 25

Eliminating Distractions

In today's society, there are innumerable distractions for a youth football player. Video games, social media, pets, academics, books, music, homework, siblings, grandparents, movies, religion, charity, politics, television, the news, etc. The list goes on and on. Some may look at many of these interests as harmless hobbies or essential components of a "well-rounded" life, whatever that means. I, however, view them as what they are—distractions that do nothing more than take the player's focus away from football. A championship coach must figure out how to eliminate these distractions.

Video games are an easy one, because most parents don't want their kids playing video games anyway. I have an absolute ban on video game playing, and violators have an old video game controller duct taped to their hands for an entire week of practice. Pets are a little more tricky. Most parents and players initially balk when I tell them they have two options—dropping off their dog at the humane society or quitting the team. But pets can be a distraction, and the last thing I need is to have a season go down the drain because some dog mistook my quarterback's arm for a squirrel. Yes, I've had players sob and refuse to speak for weeks after the pet was taken away. But in the end, a championship ring will far outlast any pet, with the possible exception of those huge tortoises that live for hundreds of years.

Homework is a tough one. I can't outright ban it, because if the players fail, they won't be eligible to play. But a "Gentleman's C" is good enough for jazz, so I make all parents agree that eighty-five percent of the time that is normally allotted for homework will instead be devoted to studying the offensive or defensive playbook. I also forbid the players from engaging in any of the following activities during the season: attending weddings or other family functions, visiting grandparents, reading books, watching or reading the news, or being within a twenty-foot radius of younger siblings.

Chapter 26

Winning a Bench Trial

If they ever decide to wise up and allow people without law degrees on the Supreme Court, my DC would be an excellent choice. While many companies and individuals waste millions of dollars each year on lawyers, my DC has demonstrated that skilled advocates like himself don't need representation.

He was arguably in need of legal counsel following our twenty-year high school reunion last summer. The reunion was held at a country club, and my DC was arrested for crack blocking some poor soul on the squash court in the middle of a match. He mistakenly thought the squash player had called to have his Chrysler LeBaron towed out of a parking spot reserved for elderly club members. My DC decided to represent himself and waive his right to a jury trial. I attended the bench trial, and what transpired was the greatest courtroom performance this side of Atticus Finch.

During the State's opening statement, my DC interposed a variety of objections that, frankly, didn't make a whole lot of sense. He went on tangents about the hearsay rule, removal to federal court, and the *Daubert* standard for expert testimony. The judge and the prosecutor both tried to tell him it's not customary to object during opening statements and that his objections were incoherent, but to no avail. The judge also had to instruct the bailiff to confiscate my DC's cell phone after he made a couple of phone calls during the prosecutor's opening statement.

My DC's opening statement was a rambling diatribe about how the entire event stemmed from the fact that he was wrongfully passed over for defensive player of the year his senior year of high school, despite leading the region in tackles. The judge asked him on several occasions to stop using profanity and barking at the prosecutor.

The State opened its case by calling this guy Steve to testify. We went to high school with Steve, and he was an eyewitness to the events at the reunion. However, Steve also was the football player who was named defensive player of the year our senior year, which prompted my DC to drop out of school. Steve's direct testimony about the incident was boring and straightforward.

My DC's cross-examination of Steve, on the other hand, was a sight to behold. He started off by asking Steve a series of questions about their respective senior seasons. When Steve claimed to have led the team in tackles, my DC pulled a football program out of his shirt (I mean that literally) and slammed it on witness stand. The prosecutor complained she hadn't been given the program ahead of time. My DC responded that he was about to "impeach the bejesus" out of Steve unless the prosecutor agreed that the court could "take judicial notice" of his high school statistics. He then started reading (in truth, shouting) his statistics into the record while the judge tried to resolve the dispute.

By the time Steve left the stand, nearly three hours had passed and it was time for lunch. My DC promised the judge that the "smoking gun" would come to light in the afternoon, when he would be "aggressively cross-examining" himself. The judge announced we would reconvene in an hour, but begged the prosecutor to "please, for the love of God, try and work something out with this man so we can stop this." The prosecutor ended up just agreeing to drop the charges in exchange for my DC agreeing not to set foot in that country club ever again.

In short, justice prevailed.

Chapter 27

Punishing Poor Play

As discussed above, I have no shortage of drills to deploy when I want to make a player quit. But what about when I don't want a player to quit, but I need to punish him for poor play? That requires more creativity.

I am a big believer in the old mantra that "the punishment should fit the crime," so I try to make sure to tailor the punishment to the mistake itself. You drop a pass or fumble? I duct tape a football to your hands and make you carry it around at school. You miss a block and cause my quarterback to get sacked? I put you at quarterback, make you stand there with your arms in the air, and let the actual quarterback hit you at full speed. You run the wrong route at receiver? I make you run what I like to call the "Never-ending Out Route," which just consists of running in a ten-yard by ten-yard square for the entire practice. You show up thirty minutes late for practice? I make you spend thirty minutes hitting the blocking sled the next morning so that you show up to school thirty minutes late. An eye for an eye.

I'm a big fan of public humiliation. We once had a defensive back on our youth football team that my DC could not stand. We drafted him in the early rounds, but he proved to be a major bust. When he gave up a touchdown pass during one game, my DC wrote "Ryan Leef" (yes, that's how he spelled it) in permanent marker on the back of his jersey and made him backpedal around the field until the game ended. I also have a custom-made dunce cap that says "Dumbass of the Week." Each week, I give it to the player who made the most boneheaded play in the game and make him wear it to school, around town, and wherever else he goes for the next seven days.

Ultimately, these are all essential tools for getting the best out of your players. Really, they are acts of caring.

Chapter 28

Criticizing Local High School Athletes on Social Media

As you should know by now, I am a man who both supports his high school football program and demands excellence in all aspects of life. Given this, it shouldn't come as a surprise that I hold high school athletes to the same standard as my youth football players. And that means calling out poor play when I see it.

A few years ago, my high school got embarrassed by our biggest rival in the last football game of the year and missed the playoffs. I'd been running my mouth all week on Facebook to people who attended the rival school, only to watch of bunch of high school players go out and sleepwalk through the game.

I'd been stewing about the loss the entire week after the game. But the final straw came when the local paper ran this ridiculous puff piece lauding the team because every senior had already been accepted to college. There was nary a mention of the team's complete pants-shitting performance against our rival. So I decided to take matters into my own hands.

I took a picture of my region championship ring (three-way tie), posted it to Facebook, and tagged several of the high school players. I told them I hoped their college acceptance letters were keeping them company at night while they were sitting at home and missing the playoffs with the knowledge that they'll never brandish a championship ring like me. I called them an embarrassment to the community and demanded a public apology.

You'd think I tried to burn down the school. Within a few hours, my Hotmail inbox was flooded with a bunch of messages from angry parents who claimed they were going to try to get me banned from all games in the future. I guess that's just the world we live in today where a person who demands excellence and commitment is branded as a pariah.

America, 2018, ladies and gentlemen.

Made in the USA
Columbia, SC
06 July 2022

62943227R00052